Mixtures and Solutions

Developed at
Lawrence Hall of Science
University of California at Berkeley

Published and Distributed by **Delta Education**

ISBN 10: 1-58356-845-X
ISBN 13: 978-1-58356-845-3
542-2024

6 7 8 9 10 11 12 QUE 12 11 10 09 08 07

TABLE OF CONTENTS

MIXTURES AND SOLUTIONS

The next time you are enjoying yourself at a beach, pick up a handful of sand and look closely at it. You might see many different tiny rocks or pieces of seashells. Some might be red, yellow, black, white, pink, gray, or other colors. The handful of sand is a *mixture* of several different things.

Mixtures are everywhere, but most people don't notice them. The sidewalk you walk on is a mixture. Look at it with a hand lens. You might be surprised at what you see. Look in your desk. The contents may be a mixture of school papers, pencils, dust, paper clips, or other things. The bag of mixed nuts that you eat as a snack is a mixture. A cup of vegetable soup is a mixture of peas, carrots, potatoes, and perhaps beans or celery. Any time two or more different objects or materials are put together or combined, they form a mixture.

You can make mixtures yourself. You can make your own mixture of nuts if you have several different kinds, such as pecans, cashews, and sunflower seeds. Or you can chop up several kinds of lettuce, some tomatoes, and maybe a cucumber to make a mixed salad. What do you think salad dressing is? That's right, it's a mixture. A salad dressing might be a mixture of vinegar, olive oil, salt, pepper, and herbs such as rosemary and oregano. And if you ate some nut mix, followed by some vegetable soup and salad with dressing, just think about the mixture in your stomach!

Some mixtures are made by combining solids and liquids. You might have started your day with a mixture of cereal, milk, and sugar. Or maybe you ate pancakes made with flour and milk. Did you ever mix cocoa powder (a solid) with milk (a liquid) to make chocolate milk? That's another tasty mixture.

What Is It?

Can you guess what these photographs are? Are they mixtures or solutions?

Sand

Granola

Tea

Sometimes when you mix a solid and a liquid, an interesting thing happens. The solid material seems to disappear. If you ever put sugar in iced tea or lemonade powder in a glass of water, you probably noticed this happen. The sugar or powder went to the bottom of the glass, but after a bit of stirring, you could not see it. When a solid material seems to disappear in a liquid, the mixture is called a *solution*. Solutions are always clear. You can see through solutions. A solution can be colored, like iced tea or lemonade, but it must be clear. Do you think chocolate milk is a solution?

When a solid disappears in a liquid, we say the solid has *dissolved* in the liquid. The scientific names for the solid and liquid are *solute* and *solvent*. If you mix salt and water, the salt is the solute. It dissolves in the solvent, which is the water.

Substances in solutions are so tiny that you can't see them. You can't see a spoonful of sugar or salt in water, but you know it is there because you can taste it. Substances can be made smaller and smaller until they are invisible to your eyes.

A solution isn't always made with a solid and a liquid. Solutions can be made with two liquids. Corn syrup can dissolve in water. Liquid detergent can also dissolve in water. Which liquid do you think is the solvent, and which is the solute? Solutions can also be made with liquids and gases. Carbon dioxide is dissolved in water to put the fizz in soda drinks.

The air you breathe is a solution. It is a mix of different gases dissolved in nitrogen. When gases from vehicles and particles of dust and dirt are added to the air in large quantities, we call the air *smog*. Some people have difficulty breathing very smoggy air.

A smoggy day in Los Angeles

The First 30 Elements

The following list shows the first 30 elements, ordered from the lightest to the heaviest atoms. Look at the list to answer the following questions.

- What is the lightest atom on the list? The heaviest on the list?
- Is aluminum heavier or lighter than titanium?
- Is iron heavier or lighter than titanium? Than aluminum?
- The air we breathe is mostly a mixture of oxygen and nitrogen. The amount of nitrogen in the air is four times greater than the amount of oxygen. Which of these two elements is the lighter?
- Argon, neon, oxygen, fluorine, nitrogen, chlorine, and helium are all gaseous elements. Put these seven gases in order from lightest to heaviest.
- Iron, aluminum, nickel, titanium, chromium, copper, zinc, and cobalt are all metal elements. Put these eight metals in order from lightest to heaviest.

1 Hydrogen	**11** Sodium	**21** Scandium
2 Helium	**12** Magnesium	**22** Titanium
3 Lithium	**13** Aluminum	**23** Vanadium
4 Beryllium	**14** Silicon	**24** Chromium
5 Boron	**15** Phosphorus	**25** Manganese
6 Carbon	**16** Sulfur	**26** Iron
7 Nitrogen	**17** Chlorine	**27** Cobalt
8 Oxygen	**18** Argon	**28** Nickel
9 Fluorine	**19** Potassium	**29** Copper
10 Neon	**20** Calcium	**30** Zinc

Mixtures can be taken apart. You can clean up your drawer and put things in their proper places. You can separate your handful of sand into the different kinds of materials in the mixture. You can separate the kinds of nuts in your snack to eat each type one at a time.

Mixtures that are solutions can also be taken apart. Ocean water is a solution of salt and water (and often other minerals). To separate salt from a saltwater solution, all you have to do is let the water *evaporate*. When it does, the salt will be left. Most solutions can be separated by evaporation.

All solid objects on Earth can be broken down or worn down into smaller and smaller pieces. Mountains are mixtures of rocks and minerals. River bottoms are mixtures of smaller rocks and minerals that have been worn away from mountains and other places. River sand is a mixture of even smaller rocks and minerals. River silt is a mixture of very tiny rocks and minerals.

Today we know that some substances on Earth are not mixtures. They are called *elements*. Gold is an element. No matter how you break up gold, all the pieces are still gold, even down to the tiniest pieces. Copper is another element. So are oxygen and helium. Ninety-two different elements are found naturally on Earth. Everything on Earth is made out of one or more of these elements.

For many centuries, people wondered how small the smallest piece of something could be. Scientists have given a name to the tiniest piece of an element. The tiniest piece is called an *atom*. Gold is made up of gold atoms, and copper is made up of copper atoms. Oxygen atoms make up the oxygen in the air we breathe. We use helium atoms to fill balloons. Atoms are so small that you can't see them. It takes about 1 million copper atoms to make a tiny, visible piece of copper. It would take 39 million copper atoms side by side to make a line 1 centimeter (one-half inch) long.

Scientists have put the 92 natural elements in order from the lightest to the heaviest. The first element is hydrogen. It is the lightest and the most common element in the universe. The Sun is made up mostly of hydrogen. On Earth, hydrogen is a gas. It is used as rocket fuel.

Element 2 is helium. It is the next lightest atom. Helium is also a gas. Because it is lighter than air, it is used to fill blimps and party balloons.

The Amazing Atom

The idea of the atom was conceived by Greek philosophers more than 2,000 years ago. They thought that if something was cut into smaller and smaller pieces, eventually it would be divided into pieces too small to cut. They called these pieces *atoms*. Atom comes from the Greek word *atomos*, which means "that which cannot be cut."

Atoms are so small that you can't see them directly. Just how small are they?

- One drop of water contains more than 100,000,000,000,000,000,000 (100 billion billion) atoms.
- It would take all the people in the world all their lifetimes to count the number of atoms in one letter on this page.

What element was used to fill this blimp?

SUPER SCIENTISTS

Henry Cavendish
(1731–1810)

English chemist Henry Cavendish is most famous for his study of the composition of air. He showed that air is a mixture of more than one gas. He was the first person to isolate hydrogen from air. He called it "inflammable air" because it seemed to burn easily. Cavendish was also the first to find that water is made up of two elements, hydrogen and oxygen.

Henry Cavendish

Element 8 is very important. It is oxygen. It is part of the solution we call air. Humans and other animals take in oxygen when they breathe. You need oxygen to stay alive. Nearly all organisms need it to survive.

Element 26 is iron. When you see red-colored hillsides or mountains, it is likely that they contain iron. People found that they could remove iron from the mixture of red dirt using heat. They could melt the iron and form it into different shapes. For many centuries, iron has been a very useful element for making tools.

A landscape made red by iron at Valley of Fire State Park in Nevada

The manufacture of iron by the petroleum process, from 1880

Iron-Bound Mallets

Iron-ring mallet

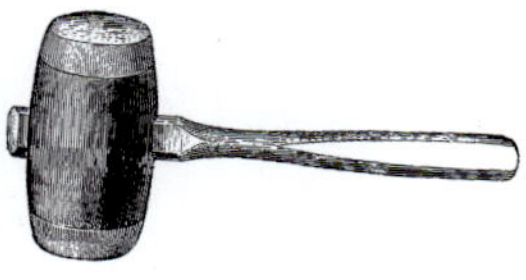

Round iron mallet

Interesting stories can be told about each of the 92 elements. Each has been useful in some way to humans. *Chemists* study the elements. They study how elements can be combined and how elements and their combinations can be used. Chemists will have plenty to do for a long time, because there are many things still to be learned about elements.

QUESTIONS TO EXPLORE

- What are some examples of mixtures?
- How can mixtures be separated?
- What is an element?

Atom Symbols

People use abbreviations or symbols to stand for things or ideas. The names of states are represented by abbreviations. New York, for example, can be represented by the abbreviation NY. TX is the abbreviation for Texas. CA is the abbreviation for California. What is the abbreviation for the state in which you live?

Atoms are represented by symbols. O is the symbol for oxygen. N is the symbol for nitrogen. I is the symbol for iodine.

Some names of atoms begin with the same letters, so the same symbol cannot be used for both. This is why the hydrogen symbol is H, and the helium symbol is He. C is carbon, while Ca is calcium.

In early times, Romans and Greeks used substances such as gold, silver, and iron to make art objects and tools. They used words in their own languages to name the substances. The Latin word for gold is *aurum.* Silver was called *argentum.* Iron was called *ferrum.* Today the atoms for these elements are given the symbols Au, Ag, and Fe.

Take some time to look at the periodic table that lists the 92 natural elements (see page 36). See if you can find other symbols that come from Roman or Greek words.

Athena, the Greek goddess of wisdom, wearing a crown of gold

A SALTY STORY

Most people don't notice it, but salt is everywhere. It is in most of the foods you eat. It is used in cooking and at the table to improve the flavor of foods. Salt is found in ocean water. There are places on land where great deposits of salt are found. The salt flats near Salt Lake City, Utah, are one example. That salt was left behind when sea water evaporated a very long time ago.

A salt flat in winter

Salt has been important to people since early times. It was often used to keep food from spoiling. Heavily salted food could be preserved for a long time. When sailors spent months at sea, the foods they carried on their ships were heavily salted.

Salt is the oldest known food additive. The earliest reference to salt was written in China around 2700 B.C.E. It described how salt made food taste better and helped people stay healthy.

The value of salt led to the development of a salt industry. Salt was first mined from salt deposits on land. It was packaged and sold or traded in marketplaces. In Europe, some monarchs placed heavy taxes on salt. In France, the salt tax was one of the reasons for the French Revolution in 1789.

Salt was important in United States history, too. The first patent issued to a U.S. colonist by the British government was for a salt making process. The process involved boiling sea water in huge iron pans. As the water boiled away, the salt was left in the pans. The U.S. salt industry continued to grow. Salt became one of the main products shipped along the Erie Canal in the 1800s. And during the Civil War (1861–1865), Union forces attempted to destroy the South's salt industry. They did not want the South to be able to preserve food for its soldiers.

Today more uses have been found for salt. It is added to the diets of livestock to improve their health. It is used to soften hard water. It is used to melt ice on slippery roads. And other chemicals are produced from salt, such as chlorine and sodium.

WHAT IS SALT?

Look at a tiny piece of salt. You will see that it appears to be a cube-shaped crystal. Chemists describe salt as a *compound.* A compound is a substance that is made up of two or more elements. Salt is made up of sodium (Na) and chlorine (Cl). The chemists' name for salt is *sodium chloride.* The formula chemists give this compound is NaCl.

Neither sodium nor chlorine is found in nature by itself. In 1807, English scientist Humphry Davy found a way to separate the two elements that make up salt. The separation produced the element chlorine and the element sodium. This is one reason why scientists value salt. It is the major source of chlorine and sodium. These two elements are important to many industries. Chlorine is used to make medicines, pesticides, and chemicals. Sodium is used to make chemicals, soaps, medicines, and other important products.

Salt to the Rescue

In 1924, physician David Marine persuaded a group of Michigan doctors to add the element iodine to common table salt. For years, Marine had researched the cause of *goiters.* A goiter is a swelling of the *thyroid,* a gland in the neck. Marine determined that goiters were caused by a lack of iodine in the diet. He thought that by adding iodine to something as widely used as salt, goiters could be wiped out.

Marine was right. By 1951, iodized salt had all but ended iodine deficiency problems in the United States. People in other parts of the world do not get enough iodine. They continue to suffer from goiters. The World Health Organization hopes that iodized salt can help developing countries. The organization intends to end iodine deficiency problems in Africa, Asia, and Latin America.

Salty Facts

- Salt makes up 77 percent of all the minerals in ocean water. It is estimated that there are about 45 million billion tons (50 million billion English tons) of salt in the sea.
- Ancient Greeks traded salt for slaves. Slaves were "not worth their salt" if they didn't work hard.
- Roman soldiers were paid part of their wages in salt. The Latin for these salt rations, *salarium argentum,* is the root of the English word "salary."
- An adult human body contains about 250 grams (8.75 ounces) of salt.

Making and Mining Salt

One of the earliest ways people made salt was by boiling sea water. When the water boiled away, it would leave behind the salt. In North America, hundreds of years before colonists arrived, Native Americans boiled sea water to get salt.

The production of salt was important to colonists in the 1700s. After boiling away the water, workers packed the salt into molds to dry. When dry, the salt was sold as lumps in the shapes of the molds.

By the late 1800s, factories used huge vacuums to separate sea water into salt and water. Today the vacuum pans are large, airless, enclosed cylinders that more quickly and effectively evaporate water. This method is presently the most common way to obtain salt. Most of the table salt in the United States is produced in this way.

Another early way people produced salt was to dig it right out of the ground. Land deposits of salt were sometimes found on or near the surface. That salt could be dug up in much the same way as any other mineral deposit. If the salt deposit was far below the surface, workers tunneled to it. When they reached the salt, they carried it away like miners mine other earth materials. One of the earliest salt mines on record was established in Poland around 1251. The salt that comes from mines is called *rock salt.*

SUPER SCIENTISTS

Robert Boyle
(1627–1691)

Robert Boyle was an Irish-born scientist. He is considered the "father of chemistry." He thought human knowledge could be improved through experimentation. He did many experiments with gases and founded procedures for isolating and collecting gases.

Salt and Folklore

Because of its importance to people of different cultures, many stories have been made up about salt.

- After you spill salt, throw a pinch of it over your left shoulder to avoid bad luck.
- In the 1800s, people in such countries as Scotland and Ireland thought salt would bring health to a newborn baby. To ensure good health, they placed salt in the baby's pockets or bathed the baby in salt water.
- Newlyweds in Poland are given gifts of salt and bread after their marriage for health and good fortune.
- At medieval feasts, important people were seated closer to the salt than less important people. This gave rise to the saying, "Above the salt."
- Long ago, sailors thought it bad luck to mention salt at sea. In some places, this superstition lasted as long as the 1930s.
- In Japan, salt was once sprinkled on theater stages to keep evil spirits from bewitching the actors.

SUPER SCIENTISTS

Marie Curie

(1867–1934)

Marie Sklodowska Curie was a Polish-born French scientist. She overcame prejudice and discrimination in the male-dominated world of science. She made important contributions in the fields of chemistry and physics. Along with her husband Pierre, Curie discovered the elements radium and polonium in 1898. The Curies also conducted important research on radioactivity. Curie was awarded the Nobel prize twice, first in 1903 and again in 1911. In 1934, she died from an illness caused by exposure to radioactive materials.

Marie Curie

EARTH ELEMENTS

Everything is made of atoms, including you. That means you are made of elements in the periodic table. How many of the 92 elements do you think it takes to make a person?

You probably have a trace amount of every element in your body. That's because elements are found everywhere in our environment, including our air, water, and food. For instance, helium is in the air in tiny amounts. Small amounts of helium enter our bodies when we breathe. Lead gets into the water and air, and then into our bodies. It can poison us if we get too much. Some elements are essential for life. We need tiny amounts of some, like chlorine and iodine, but large amounts of others, like carbon and oxygen.

The human body is about 75 percent water. Water is made from the elements hydrogen and oxygen.

Much of the rest of the body is made from the element carbon combined with oxygen and hydrogen. These three elements form carbohydrates (sugars and starches), lipids (oil and fats), and proteins. The soft parts of the body, like skin, muscle, fat, and organs, are made of carbohydrates, lipids, and proteins. Proteins also contain nitrogen.

The tough, rigid parts of the body, like teeth, bones, and cartilage, are rich in calcium. Blood contains a lot of iron. Potassium and sodium are needed for nerve and brain function.

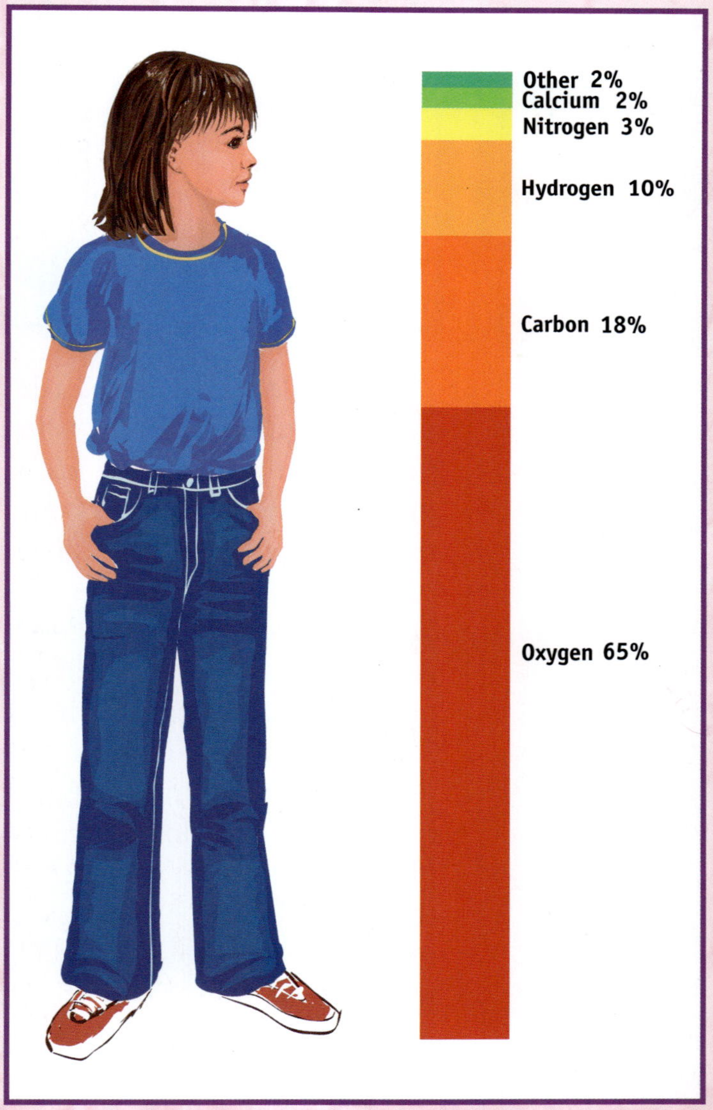

When you add it all up, about 98 percent of the human body is composed of only five elements. They are oxygen, carbon, hydrogen, nitrogen, and calcium. The remaining 2 percent is small amounts of a lot of different elements.

Most organisms are chemically very similar to humans. So it's pretty safe to say that all life is based on the same five elements. And anything we use that comes from organisms, such as wood, paper, cotton, fabrics, plastics, food, and fuels, will also be made out of these five elements.

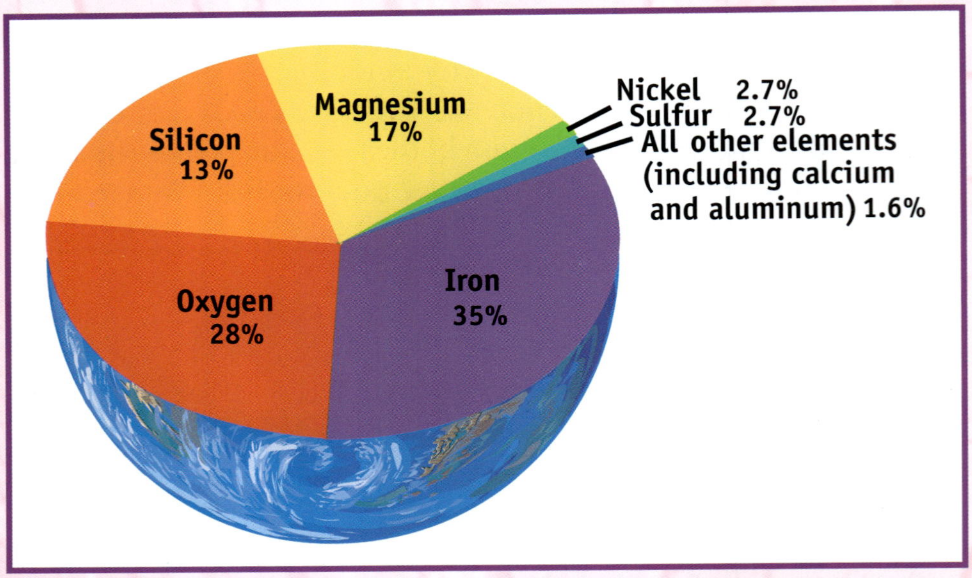

On a larger scale, Earth itself is made out of elements. The most abundant element is iron (35 percent). The massive core of the planet is mostly iron. Next are oxygen (28 percent), magnesium (17 percent), and silicon (13 percent). These are the main elements in minerals and rocks. They make up the largest part of the planet, the mantle and crust. The other major elements that make up Earth are nickel (2.7 percent), sulfur (2.7 percent), calcium (0.6 percent), and aluminum (0.4 percent). The other 84 elements together make up a tiny 0.6 percent of Earth. This includes the oceans and atmosphere.

It might seem that Earth is a pretty simple place. It's made mostly out of a dozen or so elements. But Earth is not a simple place. It is not the number of different elements that determines the complexity of things. It's the ways the elements bond together into molecules. These few elements can combine to make millions of different materials. That's where the wonderful variety on Earth comes from.

DECOMPRESSION SICKNESS

Our bodies are under pressure all the time. The air around us has mass, and that mass pushes on our bodies. If you have ever flown in an airplane or traveled up a high mountain, you might have noticed changing pressure in your ears. The higher you go above sea level, the less air there is pushing on you. Ears have the ability to balance the pressure inside them so it is the same as the outside pressure.

Small amounts of the gases in air are dissolved in fluids in our bodies. One of the gases, nitrogen, causes problems if the pressure on our bodies is first increased and then decreased. Here's how that works.

When we breathe, we take in oxygen and nitrogen from the air. In our lungs, the oxygen and nitrogen dissolve in our blood. Nitrogen dissolves in the blood until the blood is saturated. Under normal pressure, the blood saturated with nitrogen is no problem. When the air pressure is decreased, the blood can no longer hold all the nitrogen, and it is released as gas bubbles.

The amount of nitrogen that will dissolve in blood depends on the pressure. The greater the pressure, the more nitrogen dissolves in your blood. Can you figure out what happens to the nitrogen when the pressure goes down?

If you fly in an unpressurized airplane, the decrease in pressure as you fly higher causes the dissolved gases in your blood to come out of solution. If the airplane climbs slowly enough, the gases have time to come out through your bloodstream slowly, and your lungs exhale the gases. If the airplane climbs too quickly and the pressure drops too fast, the nitrogen comes out of solution as bubbles in your bloodstream. The result is difficulty with muscle coordination, a nauseous feeling, and speech defects. If the bubbles accumulate in the joints, the pain is very severe. Bubbles trapped under the skin cause a red rash and make the skin feel itchy.

This sickness most often happens to deep-sea divers. As divers descend into the water, the pressure increases. The longer a diver stays down or the deeper the dive, the more nitrogen dissolves in the diver's body. When the diver comes to the surface, he or she might have to stop several times on the way up. If the diver is brought up too quickly, bubbles will

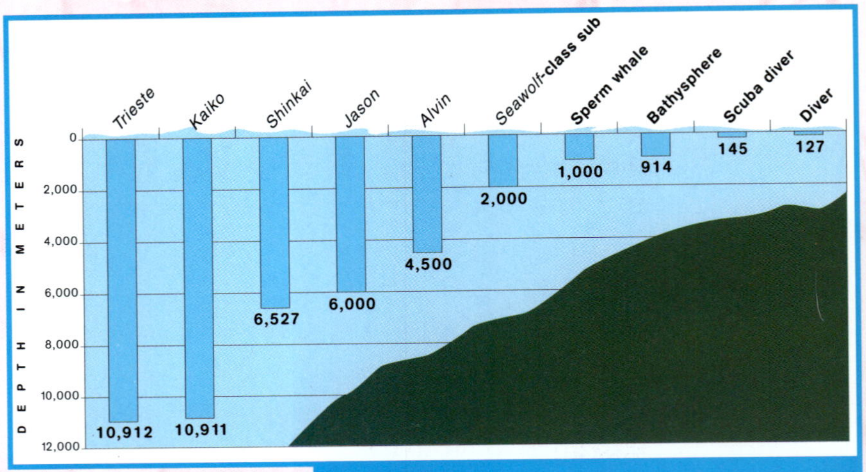

How Low Can We Go?

The deeper one goes in the ocean, the greater the pressure. In recent years, scientists have designed research vessels with thick, strong hulls to withstand the pressure. These have allowed humans to see the deepest, darkest regions of the ocean. How deep have we gone? (All depths shown are maximum depths.)

form in the blood. The diver's body may shake uncontrollably. He or she may throw up. The diver will feel pain in the joints and be unable to straighten them out. If the bubbles form in the brain, the diver might become paralyzed. This sickness is serious. It is called *decompression sickness,* or "the bends." Relief from decompression sickness is achieved by putting the person in a pressure chamber, increasing the pressure, then releasing the pressure very slowly. This process does not always reverse the damage done to the body tissues.

Today divers who venture far below the sea's surface use computers. These computers tell divers at what depths to stop on the way up and for how long in order to prevent decompression sickness.

CAISSON DISEASE AND TWO FAMOUS BRIDGES

One of the first reported cases of decompression sickness was not reported by divers, but by 19th-century bridge workers. In 1869, James Buchanan Eads began building a huge railroad bridge to span the Mississippi River at St. Louis.

Eads was the first American engineer to use *caissons* to build his bridge. Eads's caissons were huge, watertight, floorless steel boxes. The caissons slowly sank to the bottom of the

The Eads Bridge

river as a big concrete pier was built on top. As they sank, pressurized air was pumped into the caissons to keep the water out.

Once the caissons hit the bottom, workers could enter through the pier and an airlock on top. Once inside, the men began digging out the riverbed. Slowly the caissons and the pier on top sank lower and lower into the riverbed.

As the Eads Bridge caissons sank, the air pressure increased inside. After they came up from the caissons, workers complained of pains in their bodies. They couldn't stand up straight. The workers began calling their sickness "the bends." Doctors named the sickness "caisson disease." By the time the bridge was finished, 14 men had died from caisson disease. It was not until 1878 that French scientist Paul Bert explained the actual cause of the sickness, which was nitrogen bubbles in the blood.

The Brooklyn Bridge in New York links Brooklyn to Manhattan. The bridge took 13 years to build. Construction of the bridge started in 1870, just 1 year after the Eads Bridge was begun. Like Eads's bridge, the Brooklyn Bridge's construction was marred by death and tragedy.

Washington Roebling watching the progress of the Brooklyn Bridge

Washington Roebling was the chief engineer of the Brooklyn Bridge project. Roebling was in charge of every part of construction. He even went deep down into the caissons of the bridge. During one of these visits, Roebling suffered from the sickness and became paralyzed. Over the next few years, he supervised construction of the bridge from his bedroom window.

Roebling was not the only Brooklyn Bridge worker who suffered from this condition. At least three workers died from decompression sickness over the course of construction, and many more were seriously ill.

SOUR POWER

Do you like it when a glass of super-sour lemonade makes your lips pucker? Do you like having a piece of sour candy that makes your eyes water? If something that leaves a sour taste in your mouth is okay with you, then you're a fan of citric acid!

Citric acid is a white, solid acid. It is also highly *soluble* in water. You can dissolve a lot of it in a small amount of water. Like other acids, citric acid has sour power. If you've ever bitten into a lemon, then you know how citric acid tastes. About 6 percent of lemon juice is citric acid. Citric acid is found naturally in other fruits such as oranges, limes, and grapefruits. All of these fruits are known as *citrus* fruits.

Citric acid is found in most plants and animals. This important acid aids the process by which living things use energy to grow and move. This process is called *metabolism*.

Citric acid is a widely used food additive. It is sour, safe, and inexpensive. Every year, tons of citric acid are added to foods. As an additive, it can be used for a number of purposes. It gives many foods their sour tastes, including sodas and candies. In jams and preserves, it helps fruits keep their color and flavor. Look on the backs of some cans and boxes in your cupboard. You will probably find a few foods that include citric acid as an ingredient. Citric acid is also used to make inks, dyes, medicines, and cleansers.

Scientists can obtain citric acid by extracting it from lemons and other citrus fruits. But because citric acid is so widely used today, huge quantities are needed. So factories have been built to obtain citric acid from fermenting sugar.

Citric acid is not the only type of acid found in foods. Other weak acids are found in such natural substances as vinegar, tomatoes, and sour milk. There are also acids unrelated to food that are stronger and can be more dangerous. They can burn through skin and paper and should be handled with care. These types of acids are often used by scientists to conduct experiments and make chemicals.

Karl Wilhelm Scheele

Karl Wilhelm Scheele did not get the fame and attention some of his peers received. Yet Scheele made many discoveries that furthered the science of chemistry. One of his discoveries was citric acid.

Scheele was a careful researcher and experimenter. However, he would often wait for a long time before writing about and publishing his results. This delay sometimes led to others getting credit for discoveries that Scheele had made.

In 1772, for example, Scheele discovered oxygen while heating potassium nitrate. The credit for this discovery eventually went to Joseph Priestley 2 years later because Priestley's account was published first. Scheele would not publish his account until 1777, which was 5 years after the event.

Among Scheele's other discoveries were the elements nitrogen, chlorine, and manganese. The Swedish chemist proved nitrogen to be a component of air. In 1785, Scheele isolated citric acid in certain plants.

Citric Acid and Your Taste Buds

How does your tongue know when something is sour or sweet? Taste buds on the top of the tongue detect different tastes. People have between 2,000 and 5,000 taste buds on their tongues.

There are four basic tastes that your tongue can detect. They are sour, sweet, bitter, and salty. Taste buds concentrated on different parts of the tongue sense the chemicals such as citric acid found in food. Then nerve cells connected to the taste buds send messages to the brain about what the chemicals taste like. Humans are more sensitive to bitter and sour tastes than to sweet and salty tastes. Both bitter and sour tastes can alert you to foods that might be harmful. Sour often means something is rotten or unripe. Bitter can mean poison.

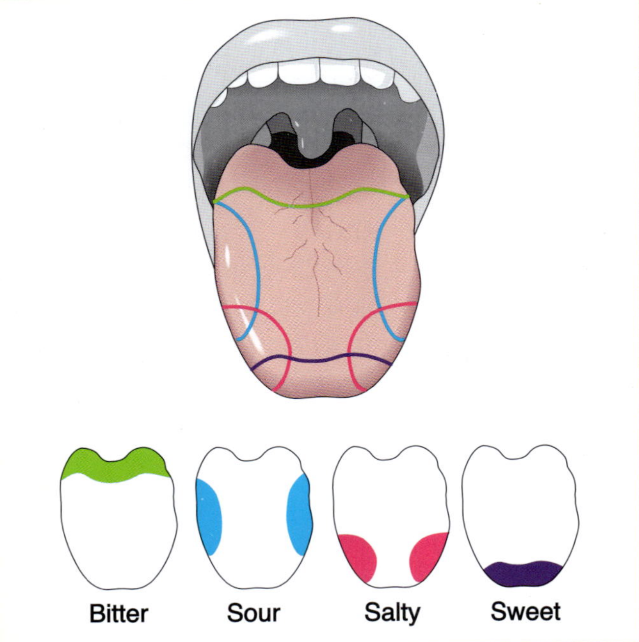

GROW YOUR OWN CRYSTALS

What happens when a solution becomes super-saturated? To find out, try this recipe for making crystals.

***Safety Note** This recipe involves boiling water and borax. Borax is a cleaning substance that can be harmful if swallowed. Please be sure to have a parent or another adult help you.

What you need

Pipe cleaners
A piece of string about 15 centimeters (6 inches) long
A pencil
Boiling water
A wide-mouthed glass jar
A tablespoon
Borax (available at a grocery store in the laundry and soap aisle)

What you do

1. Bend your pipe cleaners into any shapes you like. Try making a heart, a moon, a star, or a snowflake.
2. Tie one end of the string to the top of your shaped pipe cleaner.
3. Tie the other end of the string to the pencil. Make the string long enough so that the shape will land in the middle of the jar when the pencil is placed across the mouth of the jar.
4. Ask the adult helping you to pour boiling water into the wide-mouthed jar.
5. Add 1 tablespoon of borax to the hot water. Stir. Continue to add and stir 1 tablespoon after another. Stop when you see borax beginning to settle on the bottom of the jar. This usually takes about 3 tablespoons of borax for every 240 milliliters (1 cup) of hot water you use. Your borax and water solution is now saturated.

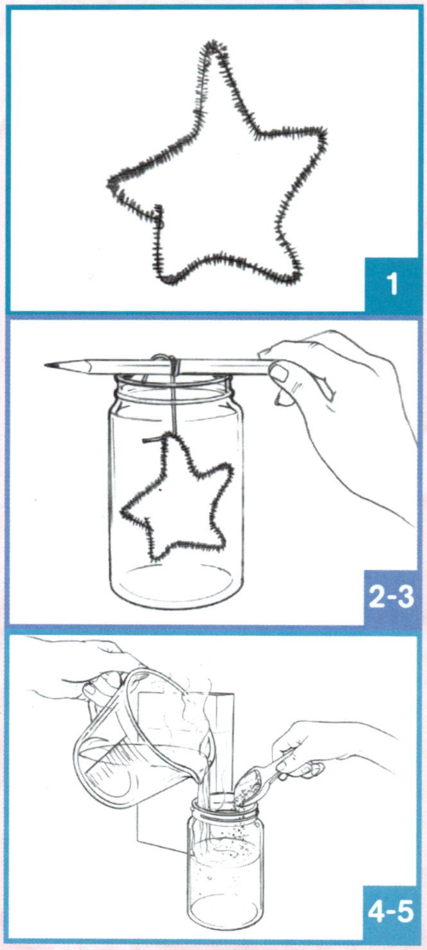

6. Lower your shape into the solution. Make sure that the entire shape is in the solution but not touching any part of the jar.
7. Rest the pencil on the mouth of the jar.
8. Allow your shape to sit in the solution overnight.
9. The next day, remove your shape. It should be covered with thick, sparkling crystals. Hang it in a spot where it can drip dry. Pour the remaining borax solution down the sink.

6-7

8-9

What happens

What's the science behind your crystals? Sometimes crystals form as saturated solutions cool.

The amount of solute that can be dissolved in a liquid depends upon two things. It depends upon the kind of solute being used and the temperature of the liquid. In general, the higher the temperature, the greater the amount of solute that can be dissolved.

But even hot water becomes saturated eventually. When the borax begins to settle on the bottom of the jar, your solution is saturated. That is, the hot water cannot hold any more borax. As the saturated solution cools, it cannot hold as much borax. The borax has to go somewhere. The pipe cleaner provides a surface on which the extra borax can be deposited in the form of crystals.

What Is Borax?

Borax is a white mineral. It forms in ancient, dried-up lakebeds. It was first used by Arabian gold- and silversmiths in the 8th century to clean the surfaces of the metals. They also used borax as a *solder,* a substance that joins two pieces of metal together. The word *borax* comes from an Arabian word that means "to glitter." Today borax is used as a water softener, cleanser, and antiseptic. It is also used to make fertilizers and medicines.

THE AIR YOU BREATHE

Have you ever been in a swimming pool that made your eyes sting and burn? If that has happened to you, there was too much chlorine in the pool water. Have you ever tasted lemonade too sour to drink? If so, the super-sour taste was because there was not enough sugar in the lemonade.

We sometimes talk about strength or weakness as one characteristic of a solution such as pool water or lemonade. We are talking about *concentration.* Concentration is the amount of a material dissolved in a liquid. The more material that is dissolved, the more concentrated the solution. We might say, for example, that the pool water had a high or strong concentration of chlorine. When talking about the lemonade, we might say that its sugar concentration was too low or weak.

WHAT IS AIR?

Air is a solution made up of oxygen, carbon dioxide, and other gases dissolved in nitrogen gas. Each type of gas is present in the air in a different concentration. The concentration of nitrogen in the air is very high. The concentration of carbon dioxide is very low.

Nitrogen makes up 78 percent of the mixture of gases we call air. It is a colorless, tasteless, odorless gas. Although we are constantly taking in nitrogen when we breathe, our bodies do not use it in any way.

Oxygen makes up about 20 percent of air. Like nitrogen, it is a colorless, tasteless, odorless gas. Animals need to breathe oxygen to survive. Every time you take a breath of air, your body keeps some of the oxygen. Oxygen travels throughout the body in the bloodstream.

Until the beginning of the 20th century, scientists believed that air was made of only nitrogen and oxygen. Then researchers began to discover more gases in air. The concentrations of these gases are very, very low. Only tiny amounts are found in air. The gases are argon, helium, krypton, neon, xenon, and radon. Like nitrogen and oxygen, these gases are colorless and odorless.

Water vapor and carbon dioxide are regularly added to the air. Water vapor is water in its gaseous form. It is added to air when water evaporates from oceans and other bodies of water. Carbon dioxide is naturally added to air when animals and humans exhale. It is also added by the decaying of dead plants and animals. Both water vapor and carbon dioxide make Earth livable. They trap heat inside the atmosphere and allow plants to grow and humans to flourish.

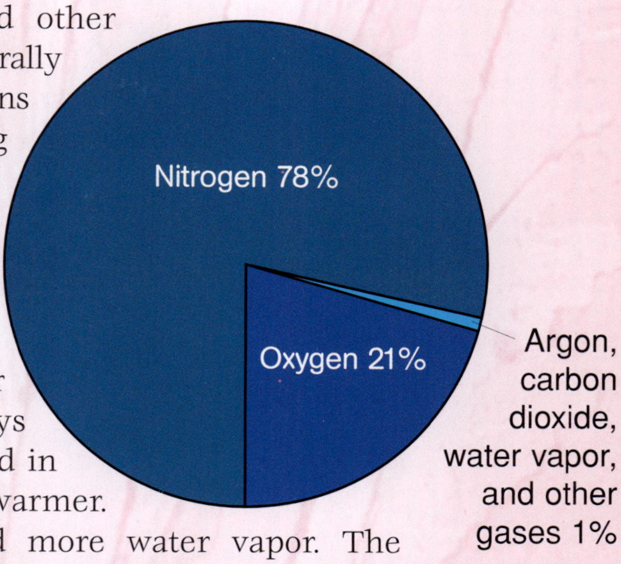

The concentrations of water vapor and carbon dioxide in the air always vary. More water vapor can be found in the air when the temperature is warmer. That's because warm air can hold more water vapor. The concentration of carbon dioxide in the air also varies from place to place and day to day.

POLLUTION IN THE AIR

Other gases and chemicals are always being added into the mixture we know as air. Some of these additions are harmful to humans, plants, and the Earth itself. Sometimes the concentrations of some particles or chemicals in the air are higher than they should be. The result is air pollution.

Even a higher concentration of something that is naturally found in the air can cause problems. For example, the concentration of carbon dioxide in the air is normally quite low. However, the burning of fossil fuels can release more carbon

The Air Astronauts Breathe

All humans must have oxygen to survive. But above Earth's atmosphere in outer space, there is no oxygen for astronauts to breathe. Space vehicles must have a way to create and keep oxygen inside, in their air supply. Systems inside the space shuttles generate and monitor oxygen and nitrogen in the air.

The concentrations of gases in the shuttles' air are nearly identical to those on Earth. Nitrogen concentration is kept at an average of 80 percent. Oxygen concentration is kept at about 20 percent. Each shuttle crew member uses about 0.8 kilograms (1.76 pounds) of oxygen each day. Oxygen and nitrogen gases also help maintain cabin pressure on board the shuttle.

A shuttle's life support must also have a system to remove carbon dioxide from the air. When people exhale, they naturally release carbon dioxide into the air. In a confined space such as the shuttle, carbon dioxide buildups can cause serious health problems. A system on board constantly filters out carbon dioxide and keeps the shuttle air healthy.

dioxide. This increases the concentration of carbon dioxide in the air. Some scientists believe that an increased concentration of carbon dioxide causes *global warming.*

Global warming is a gradual rise in the average temperature on Earth. Scientists believe it is caused by a rise in the concentration of gases in the Earth's atmosphere. These include carbon dioxide, water vapor, and other gases. As the concentrations of these gases increase, more heat is trapped near the Earth's surface.

Amazing Air Facts

- Earth's atmosphere reaches about 480 kilometers (300 miles) above sea level. It is made up of four layers. These are generally identified by differences in temperature. Humans can only breathe safely in the lowest layer, the *troposphere.* Mountain climbers sometimes venture to the top of the troposphere, 8 to 10 kilometers (5 to 6 miles) up. Then they need to carry oxygen with them.
- The next layer is the *stratosphere.* It extends from about 10 kilometers (6 miles) to about 48 kilometers (30 miles) above the Earth. Clouds are rare in this layer. Aircraft usually fly here to be above weather disturbances.
- The *ozone layer* is between the stratosphere and the *mesosphere.* The mesosphere extends to 80 kilometers (50 miles) above the Earth.
- Above this lies the *thermosphere,* where the air is very thin. Over 99.99 percent of the atmosphere lies below this layer. From here, the remaining atmosphere fades away into space.
- Air has a mass of about 1 kilogram per cubic meter at sea level.
- Earth is the only planet in our solar system that has an atmosphere capable of sustaining life as we know it. However, some people believe that the atmosphere of Mars could be altered to support life.

WHAT A REACTION!

When two or more substances are combined, changes sometimes take place. In some cases, the substances may change into a totally new product. This kind of change is a *chemical change.*

The process through which these changes take place is a *chemical reaction.* The original substances are called *reactants.* The substances that are formed by the reaction are called *products.*

A chemical reaction occurs when you combine baking soda, calcium chloride, and water. You can see the reaction taking place as the solution begins to fizz. The fizzing is actually the making of new substances. They are a gas that escapes into the air and a new white solid. Any solid produced by a chemical reaction is called a *precipitate.*

Many substances in nature are formed through chemical reactions. Water molecules, for example, are formed when hydrogen and oxygen react. Hydrogen and oxygen are the reactants, and water is the product. When sodium and chlorine react, salt (sodium chloride) forms. Sodium and chlorine are the reactants, and salt is the product.

1

Shown here are water, baking soda, and calcium chloride.

2

This is a cup of baking soda and calcium chloride mixture with a cup of water.

3

Add the water to the baking soda and calcium chloride.

4

Watch it fizz!

SLOW REACTIONS, FAST REACTIONS

Reactions occur at different rates. Some take place slowly, over long periods of time. Others happen in a split second. Rusting is one type of slow chemical reaction. It occurs when metals such as iron react with oxygen. To see the effects of another type of reaction, look at an old copper penny. The chemical reaction between copper and the oxygen in the air takes place over a long period of time. Eventually a green oxide will cover the penny's surface.

Explosions are examples of super-fast chemical reactions. Explosions occur quickly and violently. An explosive reaction occurs when hydrogen and oxygen combine or when a firecracker blows up. Air bags in cars are also inflated by a very fast-acting chemical reaction.

A number of factors can affect the speeds of reactions. One factor is temperature. Colder temperatures slow reaction times, while warmer temperatures speed reactions. Concentration also affects reactions. The greater the concentration of a mixture or solution, the faster the reaction.

SUPER SCIENTISTS

Marguerite Perey
(1909–1975)

Marguerite Perey had the good fortune to have one of the best role models in the world of chemistry, Marie Curie. Perey's first job was to work as Curie's assistant at the Radium Institute in Paris.

Even after Curie died in 1934, Perey continued her research into radioactivity. In 1939, at the age of 29, Perey discovered a radioactive element called francium.

In 1962, she became the first woman to be elected to France's Academie des Sciences.

Marguerite Perey

QUESTIONS TO EXPLORE

- **What is a chemical change?**
- **What are two examples of chemical reactions at different speeds?**
- **What can affect the speed of chemical reactions?**

WHAT IS MATTER MADE OF?

Look closely at the salt you used in the Mixtures and Solutions activities. Remember, it's a compound made of sodium and chlorine. You will see a lot of little granules. A box of salt is actually millions of tiny bits of salt. But is a granule the smallest piece of salt?

If you put one granule of salt on a hard surface and crush it with the back of a spoon, it breaks into powder. If you look at the powder under a microscope, you will see that it is broken into a million microscopic pieces of dust. But is dust the smallest piece of salt?

If you keep breaking bits of salt smaller and smaller, you will get to the smallest possible piece of salt. That smallest piece is called a *molecule.*

WHAT IS AN ATOM?

There are 92 kinds of basic materials occurring naturally in the world. These basic materials are the *elements.* Iron is one element. Carbon is another element. Oxygen, hydrogen, and gold are each different elements. The Periodic Table of the Elements is a display of all the different elements.

The smallest piece of an element is an *atom.* Elements are made out of just one kind of atom. Iron is made of iron atoms only. Carbon is made of carbon atoms only. A helium balloon contains only helium atoms, some of the lightest atoms in the world. A gold ring is made of gold atoms, some of the heaviest atoms.

All the elements are made of their own kinds of atoms. This means that there are only 92 different kinds of atoms occurring naturally on Earth. Each kind of atom has its own properties. That's why each element is different from every other element.

It's hard to describe just how small an atom is. If you put a million hydrogen atoms in a row, the row would still be too small to see. If you put 5,000 rows of a million hydrogen atoms end to end, they would make a row 1 centimeter (one-half inch) long. That's about the distance across your fingernail. It's a total of 5 trillion atoms!

In the last decade, instruments were developed that allowed scientists to take pictures of atoms for the first time. One instrument is the tunneling electron microscope. Scientists had predicted that atoms organize into patterns when they interact with each other. The images showed that this prediction was right. This image of silicon atoms shows how they are positioned in patterns that repeat. This image was taken with a scanning tunneling microscope.

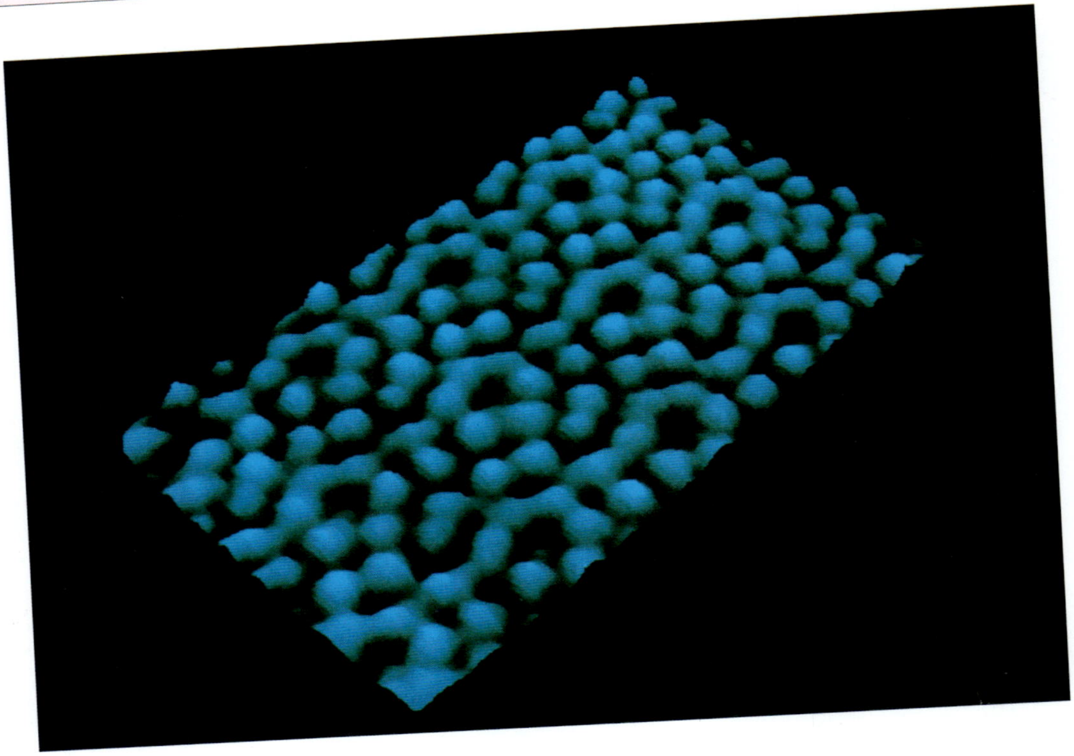

An image of silicon atoms in an organized pattern

WHAT IS A MOLECULE?

Why do we get thousands and thousands of different kinds of materials in the world if there are just a few kinds of atoms? Because different kinds of atoms can join together to form molecules. That's what a molecule is: two or more atoms attached to one another. The attachments between atoms are called *chemical bonds.*

When two or more atoms bond to form a molecule, the molecule has different properties than the atoms by themselves. Water is a molecule that forms when one oxygen atom bonds with two hydrogen atoms. Water has very different properties than the elements hydrogen and oxygen. Carbon dioxide is a molecule that forms when two oxygen atoms bond to a carbon atom. When a chlorine atom bonds with a sodium atom, a molecule of sodium chloride forms. Sodium chloride is common table salt. When you break salt into the smallest pieces that are still salt, you have molecules of sodium chloride.

A scientist working at an atomic resolution microscope

HOW DO ATOMS REARRANGE?

When atoms rearrange to form new molecules, it is called a chemical reaction. When calcium carbonate (chalk) is mixed with hydrochloric acid (stomach acid), the two materials react. The molecules in the chalk and stomach acid rearrange, and new molecules form. The reaction looks like this.

$$CaCO_3 + 2HCl \rightarrow CO_2\uparrow + CaCl_2 + H_2O$$

This is how you read the reaction.

$$Ca\ CO_3 \quad + \quad 2\ H\ Cl \quad \rightarrow \quad C\ O_2\uparrow \quad + \quad Ca\ Cl_2 \quad + \quad H_2O$$

Calcium carbonate plus hydrochloric acid yields carbon dioxide plus calcium chloride plus water.
(a gas)

In the investigation Fizz Quiz, you mixed a salt called calcium chloride with sodium bicarbonate (baking soda). When you added water, the two solid materials dissolved and reacted. New molecules formed. The starting molecules, the salt and soda, are called reactants. The new molecules are called products. In this chemical reaction, the products are carbon dioxide (a gas), calcium carbonate (a solid), and table salt (dissolved in water). The atoms in the product molecules are the same ones that were in the reactant molecules. The difference is the way the atoms are arranged. The new molecules have different properties than the molecules that reacted. When you did this reaction in a bag, the gas and the white material gave evidence that new products had formed.

$$2NaHCO_3 + CaCl_2 \rightarrow CO_2\uparrow + CaCO_3 + 2NaCl + H_2$$

All matter is made of atoms. Air, water, all the living things on Earth, and Earth itself are made of atoms. But there are only 92 different kinds of atoms. How is the huge number of different objects, materials, and organisms possible? Those atoms can bond together to form countless different molecules. And each different kind of molecule has properties that are different from the properties of every other molecule.

ASK A CHEMIST

Angelica Stacy

Beryl Baker and friend

Beryl Baker's teacher asked her sixth-grade students to do a career report for an assignment. Beryl decided to do her report on a chemist's career. To really find out what chemists do, she made an appointment to talk with Angelica Stacy, Professor of Chemistry at the University of California at Berkeley. On February 9, 1999, Beryl had this interview with Professor Stacy.

BB: *We are studying mixtures and solutions in our class. My teacher said people who work with mixtures and solutions are called* chemists. *What does it mean to be a chemist, and what does a chemist do?*

AS: That's a good question. Chemists do study mixtures and solutions, but they also study all other forms of matter, including gases and solids. We study their properties and try to find out why they do what they do. We then use that information to make new things. Chemists make many of the things around you. The material of your jacket, the dye in your jeans, medicines, plastics, and lots more.

BB: *Why do you like chemistry?*

AS: It's more that I like science, and chemistry is one piece of science. For me, chemistry is a way of thinking about the world and contributing to society at the same time.

BB: *Was there a person who started you thinking about chemistry?*

AS: My father. He was an engineer with RCA. He never got a college degree because his family was poor, so he taught himself most of what he needed to know. Because of him, there was always science in our house. He was always making things that interested me, and talking about how sound and electricity worked.

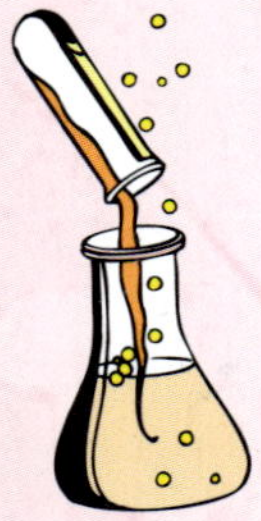

BB: *How long did you go to college to learn about chemistry?*

AS: Four years of college as an undergraduate to get my bachelor's degree, and then 4 years of graduate work to get the advanced degree so I could become a professor. In my case, it took 8 years of college-level study.

BB: *Do all chemists work at colleges or universities?*

AS: No. There is a big chemical industry worldwide. One [industry] that you probably know about is the drug companies that create and manufacture drugs to fight disease, relieve pain, treat injuries, and so on. Lots of chemists work in this industry. Chemists work in the food industry, enriching and preserving the things we eat. Agriculture depends on chemistry. All those things in the bathroom were developed by chemists: soaps and detergents, cleansers, stain removers, shampoo, hair color, mouthwash, deodorant, toothpaste. Chemists are at work in many industries and government agencies.

BB: *Does everybody who studies chemistry become a chemist?*

AS: People may use their understanding of chemistry to launch into other interesting professions. One chemist I know is now a multimedia designer. His chemistry training prepared his mind for the demanding work of creating computer programs that help students learn about science subjects in interesting and fun ways. Others might move into university administration, law enforcement, government work, medicine, or business. And many students who start in chemistry move on to other fields of science and engineering because chemistry is recognized as the basic science. Knowledge of matter and its fundamental behaviors is a good place to start with any career in science.

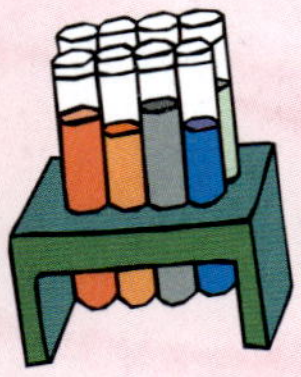

BB: *What tools and instruments do you use when you are doing your chemistry work?*

AS: We use lots of different instruments to help us find out what things are made out of and how they are put together. As it turns out, some of our most important tools use light to give us information. The way different wavelengths of light are absorbed, reflected, or changed by chemicals tells us a lot about their structure.

Separation techniques are important, too. You undoubtedly used evaporation as a way to separate a solvent from a solute in your study of mixtures and solutions. You may have used chromatography to separate the pigments in inks. We do the same kinds of things when we are confronted with complex mixtures of chemicals. This part of chemistry is called *analysis*: finding and identifying all the parts in mixtures.

BB: *Have you invented or discovered anything?*

AS: My specialty is materials. I was investigating superconductors. Superconductors conduct electricity without resistance. But now I have turned my attention to trying to develop a new kind of refrigerator. Most refrigerators today use a gas called *freon*. But there is a problem with freon. It damages the ozone layer in the atmosphere, so freon is being phased out. I'm trying to develop a solid refrigerant. When you run electricity through it, it gets hot on one end and cold on the other. Right now it is only ten percent efficient. Your freon refrigerator is 30 percent efficient. The material must get three times better to be useful on a broad scale. This is what I am trying to discover in my lab. But breakthroughs don't come easily. Discovery is hard work.

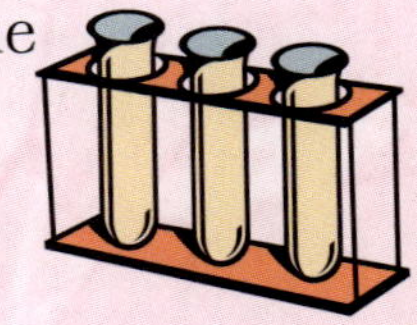

BB: *What are the most interesting things you get to do?*

AS: Teaching [is one]. My refrigeration research with graduate students is a kind of high-level teaching. I also teach basic chemistry for undergraduates, and I'm developing new ways to teach chemistry at the high school level. Another interesting part of my work is sharing ideas with other chemists all over the world. I have friends and colleagues in many countries as a result of my work in chemistry.

BB: *Is there anything else you would like to say to fifth and sixth graders about chemistry?*

AS: There are lots of opportunities in chemistry and in science generally. Whatever your interests are, knowledge of science can be part of your plans. I'd like to remind girls particularly not to be intimidated by science. In science, you have the opportunity to find things out that might help to solve problems, like my work in refrigeration, or disease control, food production, [or] lots of other things. It's a good feeling to contribute to the knowledge of the world.

THE PERIODIC TABLE

To learn more about objects, scientists often compare and sort them in various ways. Botanists sort plants on the basis of their leaves, flowers, roots, and stems. This helps them learn about plants. Geologists sort rocks and minerals based upon properties such as composition, density, and place of origin. When objects are arranged in different ways, scientists often discover patterns they might not otherwise see.

	Noms nouveaux.	*Noms anciens correſpondans.*
Subſtances ſimples qui appartiennent aux trois règnes, & qu'on peut regarder comme les élémens des corps.	Lumière	Lumière.
	Calorique	Chaleur. Principe de la chaleur. Fluide igné. Feu. Matière du feu & de la chaleur.
	Oxygène	Air déphlogiſtiqué. Air empiréal. Air vital. Baſe de l'air vital.
	Azote	Gaz phlogiſtiqué. Mofète. Baſe de la mofète.
	Hydrogène	Gaz inflammable. Baſe du gaz inflammable.
Subſtances ſimples non métalliques oxidables & acidifiables.	Soufre	Soufre.
	Phoſphore	Phoſphore.
	Carbone	Charbon pur.
	Radical muriatique	Inconnu.
	Radical fluorique	Inconnu.
	Radical boracique	Inconnu.
Subſtances ſimples métalliques oxidables & acidifiables.	Antimoine	Antimoine.
	Argent	Argent.
	Arſenic	Arſenic.
	Biſmuth	Biſmuth.
	Cobalt	Cobalt.
	Cuivre	Cuivre.
	Etain	Etain.
	Fer	Fer.
	Manganèſe	Manganèſe.
	Mercure	Mercure.
	Molybdène	Molybdène.
	Nickel	Nickel.
	Or	Or.
	Platine	Platine.
	Plomb	Plomb.
	Tungſtène	Tungſtène.
	Zinc	Zinc.
Subſtances ſimples ſalifiables terreuſes.	Chaux	Terre calcaire, chaux.
	Magnéſie	Magnéſie, baſe du ſel d'epſom.
	Baryte	Barote, terre peſante.
	Alumine	Argile, terre de l'alun, baſe de l'alun.
	Silice	Terre ſiliceuſe, terre vitrifiable.

Lavoisier's Table of the Elements

Robert Boyle (1627–1691) was an Irish chemist. He is known for his experiments with gases. He was the first person to separate and identify elements. He studied air. He found that the element oxygen was the only part of the air that was necessary for breathing and supporting life. His work founded the study of chemistry as a separate science. His clear identification of elements made it possible for the elements to be compared and sorted.

Since Robert Boyle's time, chemists have organized the natural elements of our world in different ways. An early organization of the elements was completed in 1787. Chemists ordered the elements in a line, from the lightest to the heaviest. The line was not long because at that time, scientists had isolated and described only 33 elements.

SUPER SCIENTISTS

Joseph Priestley

(1733–1804)

Joseph Priestley was a British scientist who had no formal science training. That didn't stop him from making several important contributions to the field of chemistry. In 1774, Priestley discovered oxygen. Although Karl W. Scheele had actually made the discovery 2 years earlier, Priestley was the first to publish his information. He eventually identified most of the common gases.

Joseph Priestley

NEW AND IMPROVED ARRANGEMENTS

In 1817, a German chemist named Johann Dobereiner organized the elements by their similarities. He placed all the elements that were gases in one group. In another group, he placed all the elements that were metals.

In 1864, English chemist John Newlands found that every eighth element was similar. He described this regularity as a *period.* He prepared a chart in which the elements were set in rows. Each row had eight elements. He said his chart was a *periodic* chart, or one that showed regularity from one section to another. He named his chart the Law of Octaves.

	No.		No.		No.		No.		No.		No.		No.		No.
H	1	F	8	Cl	15	Co & Ni	22	Br	29	Pd	36	I	42	Pt & Ir	50
Li	2	Na	9	K	16	Cu	23	Rb	30	Ag	37	Cs	44	Os	51
G	3	Mg	10	Ca	17	Zn	24	Sr	31	Cd	38	Ba & V	45	Hg	52
Bo	4	Al	11	Cr	19	Y	25	Ce & La	33	U	40	Ta	46	Tl	53
C	5	Si	12	Ti	18	In	26	Zr	32	Sn	39	W	47	Pb	54
N	6	P	13	Mn	20	As	27	Di & Mo	34	Sb	41	Nb	48	Bi	55
O	7	S	14	Fe	21	Se	28	Ro & Ru	35	Te	43	Au	49	Th	56

Newlands's Law of Octaves Table

MENDELEEV'S PERIODIC TABLE

As time went on, scientists discovered more elements. In 1869, a Russian chemist named Dmitri Mendeleev put together a chart showing the 63 known elements. Mendeleev's chart organized the elements by both increasing weight and similar properties. Mendeleev observed that, for his chart to make sense, he had to leave spaces between some of the elements. He believed the spaces indicated that more elements were yet to be found. The table sped the discovery of these elements by showing other scientists what properties the missing elements would have.

Mendeleev's chart is called the Periodic Table of the Elements. It is the most famous of all the ways elements have been organized. It is named the "periodic table" after Newlands's concept of a period. The elements show a repeating sequence of properties throughout the table. Elements with similar properties are positioned close to each other on the chart. In addition, Mendeleev ordered the elements by their increasing weight. Today their order is not based upon weight. They are ordered by *atomic number.* Hydrogen is 1, helium is 2, and so on. Atomic numbers tell something about the number of parts that make up an atom. Today the table contains all the known elements. You can see an updated version of Mendeleev's table on the wall of most high school science laboratories.

Reihen	Gruppo I. — R^2O	Gruppo II. — RO	Gruppo III. — R^2O^3	Gruppo IV. RH^4 RO^2	Gruppo V. RH^3 R^2O^6	Gruppo VI. RH^2 RO^3	Gruppo VII. RH R^2O^7	Gruppo VIII. — RO^4
1	H=1							
2	Li=7	Be=9,4	B=11	C=12	N=14	O=16	F=19	
3	Na=23	Mg=24	Al=27,3	Si=28	P=31	S=32	Cl=35,5	
4	K=39	Ca=40	— =44	Ti=48	V=51	Cr=52	Mu=55	Fo=56, Co=59, Ni=59, Cu=63.
5	(Cu=63)	Zn=65	— =68	— = 72	As=75	Se=78	Br=80	
6	Rb=85	Sr=87	?Yt=88	Zr=90	Nb=94	Mo=96	— =100	Ru=104, Rb=104, Pd=106, Ag=108.
7	(Ag=108)	Cd=112	In=113	Sn=118	Sb=122	Te=125	J=127	
8	Cs=133	Ba=137	?Di=138	?Ce=140	—	—	—	— — — —
9	(—)	—	—	—	—	—	—	
10	—	—	?Er=178	?La=180	Ta=182	W=184	—	Os=195, Ir=197, Pt=198, Au=199.
11	(Au=199)	Hg=200	Tl=204	Pb=207	Bi=208	—	—	
12	—	—	—	Th=231	—	U=240	—	— — — —

Mendeleev's Periodic Table of 1871

SUPER SCIENTISTS

Dmitri Mendeleev

(1834–1907)

As the youngest of 14 children growing up in Siberia, Russian chemist Dmitri Mendeleev might have been overlooked. However, his mother recognized his gift for science. When her son was 15, she took him to St. Petersburg so that he could study at the Faculty of Physics and Mathematics. In 1869, Mendeleev reorganized the known elements to make a new chart called the Periodic Table of the Elements. In addition to grouping the elements for study, the periodic table also allowed Mendeleev to predict the properties of elements undiscovered at that time.

Dmitri Mendeleev

GROUPING THE ELEMENTS

Each box in the periodic table is like a mini-biography of an element. Each box tells scientists an element's name, symbol, atomic number, and atomic weight. Scientists can also learn about an element by seeing where it is located on the chart.

In the periodic table, the rows, left to right, show the *periods.* The mass of atoms increases from left to right along a row, and the elements change from metals to nonmetals. The columns, top to bottom, are known as *groups.* The mass of atoms increases from top to bottom, and all elements in the same group have similar properties. Elements on the far right of the table, for example, are part of the family of *noble gases.* These are gases that never combine with other elements. Noble gases include helium, neon, and argon.

THE PERIODIC TABLE TODAY

After 1869, the gaps in Mendeleev's table were filled in as scientists discovered more elements. Today 112 elements appear on the periodic table. Of these, only 92 are elements that are found naturally on Earth. The others are known as "artificial elements." They are only produced in a laboratory.

Since 1900, many other ways to arrange elements have been designed. Many of them are improvements on Mendeleev's periodic table. One of the most recent arrangements is a

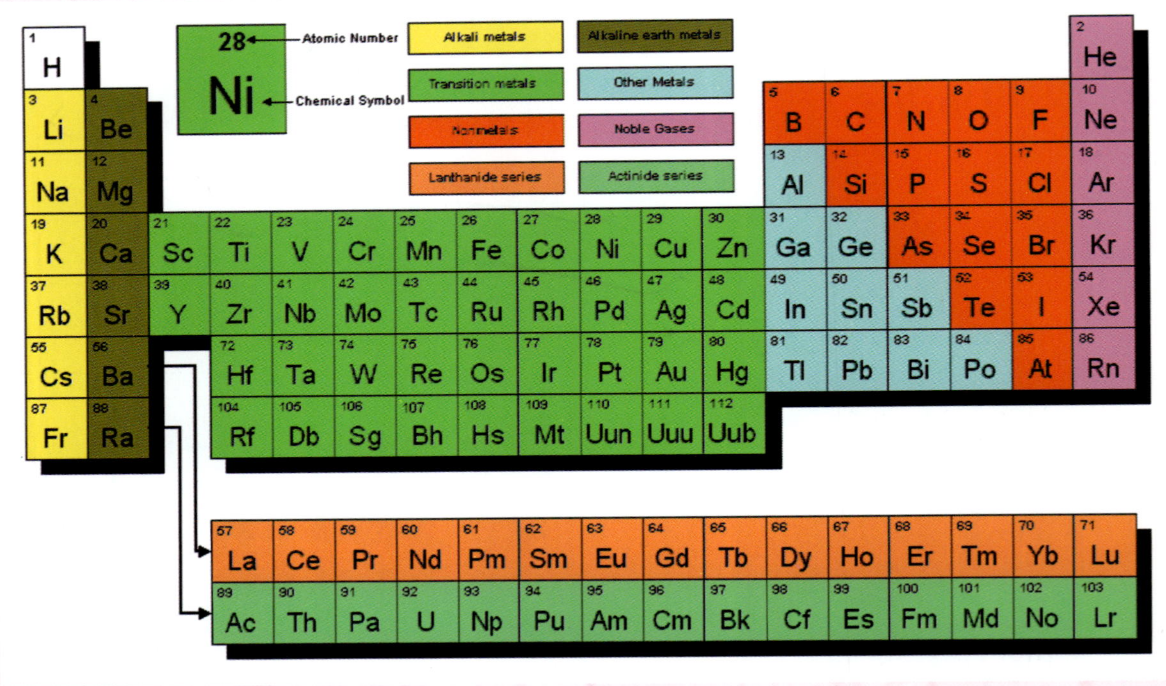

A modern Periodic Table of Elements

three-dimensional chart that displays the elements in horizontal rows and vertical columns. The chart also adds height to the boxes of the elements. The third dimension adds information about the size of the atom.

Arrangements of elements have been evolving for more than 200 years. Each has helped scientists better understand the nature of elements. Each new arrangement has improved on an earlier arrangement. Who knows? Perhaps someday you or another scientist will design another arrangement that will lead to more knowledge about the elements.

QUESTIONS TO EXPLORE

- **Whose work founded the study of chemistry?**
- **How were elements first organized in the periodic table?**
- **How is the organization of elements different today? How is it the same?**

SUPER SCIENTISTS

James Andrew Harris

(1932–)

In 1969, James Andrew Harris helped a team of Americans discover element 104. The following year, Harris also helped discover element 105. Harris, a Texas native, was working at the Lawrence Berkeley Laboratory in California when he helped make the discoveries. Element 104 (also known as rutherfordium) and element 105 (now called dubnium) are among the heaviest of all elements. They are not found outside a laboratory, however, and there is no known use for either element.

THE METALS

Look at the periodic table on page 36. The elements shown in yellow, olive, green, and blue are the *metals.* As you can see, most of the elements are metals. Metals all share a number of chemical and physical properties. Metals conduct electricity and heat well. They don't break when struck with a hammer. Most metals have shiny surfaces when rubbed or scratched.

When pure metals are found in nature, they are called *native metals.* Metals are usually found combined with other elements in rocks. Rocks that contain metals are called *ores.* Ores are processed to separate the pure metals. Metals in their elementary (pure) form have many uses.

Native copper

COPPER

Sometimes copper is found in its native form. More often it is processed from ore. Copper is widely used for electric wire and water pipes. It is used in more artistic ways, too. Did you know the Statue of Liberty is copper? The orange red color of copper changed to gray green over the years as the surface oxidized. When a metal oxidizes, oxygen from the air reacts with the pure metal to make a new molecule. The new molecule on copper is gray green.

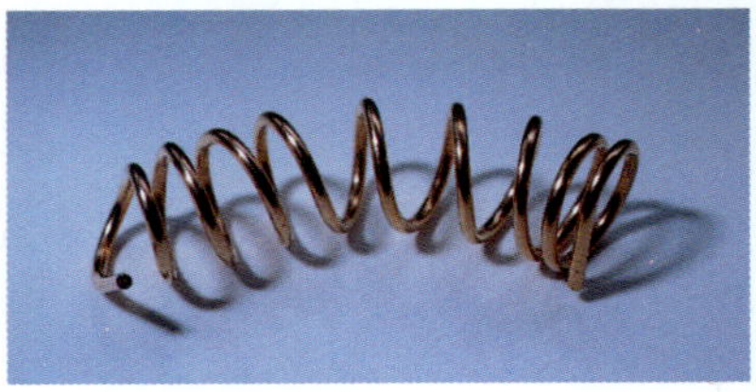

Pure copper wire

The Statue of Liberty is made of copper. Surface oxidation makes the gray green color.

ALUMINUM

Aluminum is one of the most common metals in Earth's crust, but is never found in its native form. It is mined as an ore and turned into pure aluminum *ingots* in a factory. It is then rolled flat and formed into thousands of products. Because aluminum is lightweight and tough, it is used for airplanes, backpack frames, car wheels, and cooking pots.

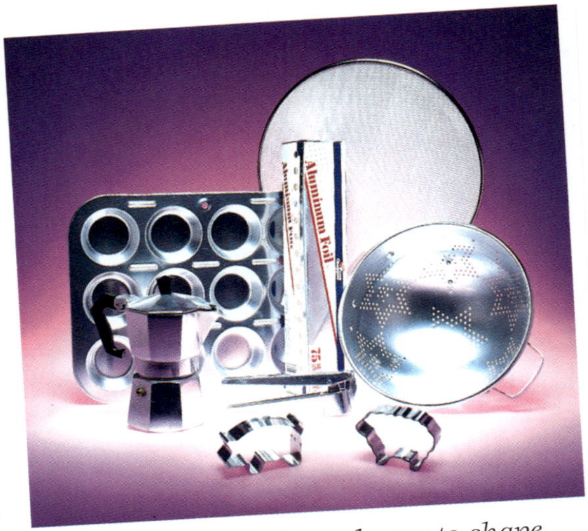

Aluminum is light and easy to shape.

Huge ingots of pure aluminum at the factory

IRON

Iron is the backbone of industry. Naturally occurring iron is brittle. But when it is treated with heat and oxygen, and mixed with small amounts of other metals, it becomes steel. Steel is strong and flexible. Huge, stable structures can be made of steel. This railroad bridge and the internal structure in the Statue of Liberty are made of steel. When iron and steel oxidize, rust forms. Oxidization slowly destroys the strength of steel, so steel structures are often painted to prevent rusting.

Native iron

Strong steel structures hold up a train bridge.

PRECIOUS METALS

Gold and silver are known as precious metals. These metals are rare. They shine with a bright luster when they are polished. They are found as native metals, but most often they are extracted from ore. Over the years, these metals have been prized for artwork and objects of status. Gold, in particular, is used for jewelry because it does not oxidize when exposed to air. Gold and silver coins are highly valued as collectors' items.

Gold objects

Native gold

Native silver

Silver objects

ALLOYS

Mixtures of metals are called *alloys.* Alloys have properties that are different from the properties of the original metals.

Different kinds of steel are made by adding small amounts of other elemental metals to iron. Each kind of steel has different properties. Chromium is added to iron to make stainless steel, which doesn't rust. Nickel is added to iron to make nickel steel, which is tough and flexible.

Some alloys have unique properties. Aluminum, nickel, and cobalt are combined to make alnico, a strongly magnetic metal.

Copper is mixed with zinc to make brass. Brass has a golden luster. It is suited for use outdoors because it resists oxidation. Copper is mixed with tin to make bronze. Bronze is a tougher, more weather-resistant metal than copper or tin alone.

Brass containers and key rings

Pure tin

Native copper

Native zinc

A bronze sculpture outdoors in a park

WHAT ARE SALTS?

Most metals dissolve in acid. When metals dissolve in acid, new molecules form. The new molecules are called *salts.* Most salts dissolve in water and conduct electricity.

Common table salt (sodium chloride or NaCl) can be made by dissolving the metal sodium in hydrochloric acid. Other salts can be produced by dissolving copper, iron, calcium, or zinc in acid. Chemists use salts to develop new molecules, like alloys, medicines, building materials, and fabrics.

Sodium chloride crystals

QUESTIONS TO EXPLORE

- **What is ore?**
- **What does oxidize mean?**
- **Why do we make alloys?**

THE HISTORY OF RUBBER

You can find it in tires, erasers, and shoe soles. It's even in wallpaper, raincoats, and parachutes. What is it? It's rubber, and it's come a long way over the past few hundred years.

There are two different types of rubber used today. They are *natural* and *synthetic.* Natural rubber is a stretchy, elastic substance. It is made by collecting rubber juice, called *latex,* from certain tropical trees. A chemical is then added to the latex to cause it to thicken and form chunks of rubber. *Crude rubber,* as the chunks are called, is white like the latex.

Synthetic rubbers are materials that, like natural rubber, are very elastic. Synthetic rubbers are made from chemicals in factories. Like natural rubber, synthetic rubber can be stretched to many times its original length. Then it will return to its original length when released. What makes rubber so stretchy? Rubber molecules are unique. They are longer and more flexible than other types of molecules.

HISTORY

Rubber has been used for centuries in some parts of the world. On one of his voyages, Columbus reported seeing the native people of Haiti playing with balls made out of rubber. Other people of the tropics also made use of rubber. To obtain the latex from rubber trees, native South Americans would slash the trees with long knives. Today trees are tapped of their sap by making a diagonal cut into the bark deep enough so that the sap runs out. A collecting trough is placed into the base of the cut. The sap runs into the trough, and from there into a collecting cup.

Tapping a rubber tree

In the late 1700s, scientists became interested in studying the properties of rubber. Joseph Priestley, best known for his discovery of oxygen, researched the properties of rubber. He gave the stretchy substance its name after noticing that rubber could rub out pencil marks.

Although scientists found rubber interesting, the tropical substance was expensive, and no one had any good use for it. Those who tried to find uses soon learned that the substance changed when the temperature changed. It became soft and sticky when hot, and hard and stiff when cold. The substance was so strange that it didn't seem to have any value at all.

AN ACCIDENTAL BREAKTHROUGH

In 1832, a struggling inventor named Charles Goodyear became fascinated with rubber. For years, Goodyear worked hard to make rubber usable. He tried mixing rubber with many different chemicals, with very little success.

Charles Goodyear

Then in 1839, Goodyear accidentally spilled a mix of rubber and sulfur onto his stove. As he cleaned up, Goodyear found that the heat had made the rubber mixture hard and durable. He had invented an important process called *vulcanization.*

In vulcanization, rubber is heated together with sulfur. A chemical reaction occurs that makes rubber strong and durable. Without vulcanization, natural rubber would not be usable.

Goodyear's discovery allowed rubber to be used in many different products. People soon began using rubber tires on automobiles. As more and more people bought cars, the demand for tires increased the demand for rubber. Today between 60 and 70 percent of all natural and synthetic rubber is used to make tires.

A tire-mounting facility in São Paulo, Brazil

SYNTHETIC RUBBER

After Goodyear's discovery, people began to depend upon rubber. During World War I (1914–1918), Germany was cut off from its rubber supply. This forced the Germans to invent a synthetic rubber, the first of its kind. During World War II (1939–1945), the United States found itself in a similar position. Scientists here began working on a good substitute for rubber. By 1945, the United States was producing 900,000 tons (1 million English tons) of synthetic rubber a year.

Most synthetic rubber today is made by combining and heating the substances styrene and butadiene. These two substances react to form a material that is very much like rubber.

Both natural and synthetic rubbers are used today. The properties of each are slightly different, so manufacturers choose one or the other, depending upon their needs. Most car tires, for example, are made of synthetic rubber. Airplane tires, however, are made from 100 percent natural rubber. Today more than two-thirds of all rubber used is synthetic.

GLOSSARY

Alloy A combination of two or more metals.
Atom The smallest particle of an element. Atoms are the building blocks of matter.
Catalyst A chemical that changes the rate of a reaction.
Chemical A substance used in chemistry.
Chemical bond The attachment between two atoms in a molecule.
Chemical reaction The process in which two or more substances combine to make one or more new substances that have different properties than the original ones.
Chemist A person trained in chemistry.
Chemistry The branch of science that deals with the composition, structure, and properties of matter.
Citric acid A white, odorless acid with a sour taste.
Compound A substance made of two or more elements that are chemically combined.
Concentration The relative amount of a substance in a mixture.
Crystal The solid form of a material that can be identified by its natural shape or pattern.
Density The ratio of the mass of a material in proportion to its volume.
Dissolving The process of a material becoming incorporated uniformly into another, or of two materials mixing together evenly.
Element A substance that cannot be broken down by simple chemical and physical processes.
Evaporate To turn into gas, like water into water vapor.
Fermenting A gradual chemical change that takes place without oxygen, caused by organisms such as bacteria or yeast.
Global warming Warming of Earth worldwide.
Ingot A mass of metal cast in the shape of a bar.
Metabolism The chemical processes that take place in a living cell or organism.
Mixture A substance containing two or more materials with different properties.
Molecule The smallest part of a substance that is made up of two or more atoms.
Periodic table An arrangement of the elements that provides information about their properties.
Precipitate A solid material that forms during a chemical reaction.
Product A new molecule created in a chemical reaction.
Reactant A chemical that takes part in a chemical reaction.
Saturated solution A solution in which as much solute as possible has been dissolved.
Soluble Capable of being dissolved. Table salt is soluble in water.
Solute A substance that dissolves in a solvent to form a solution.
Solution A special mixture formed when one or more materials dissolves in another.
Solvent A substance that dissolves a solute to form a solution.
Synthetic Something made artificially or by a laboratory chemical process, rather than by a natural process.
Vulcanization The process of treating rubber chemically in order to give it useful properties such as strength and temperature stability.